Defeating
PTSD Epidemics

Dr. Hasan Yahya

@ Hasan Yahya Publishers, USA 2012

ضمن مشروع إحياء التراث العربي في المهاجر
بدعم من الموسوعة العربية الأمريكية ومعهد التراث العربي
ومطابع القدس – الولايات المتحدة

ISBN-13: 978-1477680667
ISBN-10: 1477680667

Mental Voyage Series - 17

Manufactured in the United States of America

Preface

No body is perfect! I believe. But if you do what you love, you have to love what you do. And if you do that, then you are happy. Many people do things as if they are doing it by force. It is not important what type of force they have over them to do. But ythey have to love what they do. No matter what force they had over you you have already done it. In both cases whither the force came from a friend or not a friend. If people don't love what they do, they will feel guilty or sorry after doing what they do. If they become guilty of what they do, then it will be easy for stress to occupy their minds and their lives. In this case it is better for you to do what love, and to love what you do. Now, If you were asked this question. What is the **most important** three thing in life **make you happy the most.**? WITHOUT looking at the following list of things. What would be your answer? Reading this line will make your eyes jump directly to the list immediately, but wait a minute, give yourself a moment, and close your eyes, think of the question again, then respond to it and select the most important THREE things in your life which make you

happy. I trust you, do it right now. OK.
I am not kidding. And I am not testing
you. Because I know you're smart.
Select after you open your eyes. Write
down these selections.

1.................. 2.............
3..............

When you finish, look at the
following list and select again from the
things in it and select three from it.
You have one minute time, or two or
may be three minutes PLUS. It's OK.
Now. Set, GO.

Love	School Job,	Family
Thy Self	Nation	Auto
Money	Success	
	Friendship	
Hope	Marality	Justice
Loyalty	Trust	Honor
Health	Happiness	Travel

OK, did you finish? OK. You selected
three things from the above LIST
What are they ? write them down:

1.............. 2.............. 3.
....

Finished, OK. Now, is your selection
was from the list? You will answer:

Yes. Compare your answers between BEFORE looking at the list and AFTER you looked at the list. If your selection was from the list. Surely, you are open wide to have problems of stress, anxiety, depression, anger and fear and may be suicide later in life. I 'll call these factors from now on, the GANG FIVE Monsters (GFM), threaten your life, and I can tell you immediately that you are open to frustration and anger any time. I will tell you WHY? Before the question pop up in your mind. You may answer three options from the list, that's OK, or may not select from the list, it is also OK. If your answer was from the list or outside the list, did not include the most important thing in your life, you missed the point, because the right answer I expected from you to say: LIFE itself. If this was not among the three previous to reading the list or after reading it, .you are in trouble. Psychologically speaking. WHY? LIFE itself is the answer for those who have no windows open wide for stress or any of the GFM in their lives. Simple.

Therefore, you have to protect your life, because if you loose it, you don't need psychotherapy, you don't need to cope with the GFM, you don't need medical doctors to cure your madness or frustration, stress, anxiety, fear, anger or depression. You 've gone forever, you have no life to learn how to cope with these monsters. GOT IT. They say, the one doesn't have cannot give. And your life gives you all options in the list to be happy. It gives you love, gives you luck, money, honor, success, loyalty, family,and it gives you friendship, satisfaction, and happiness. TO BE ALIVE IS THE MOST IMPORTANT THING which makes anyone happy.

.

Seriously, if your answer was one of the above selection without including LIFE in your selection before or after reading the list, you are in trouble, and you have something the Greek philosopher Epicurus (341–270 BC) have also missed. He proposed, Pleasure as the supreme good and main goal of life but he also said, that only through self-restraint and moderation. Which gives a person the ability to tolerate frustration and discomfort which is central to stress management and PTSD diseases. See, he revised his suggestion for pleasure, and added the factor of LIFE, because if you passed away , in other words, dead, you have no self-restraint and moderation. You are dead, or don't give a damn to LIFE, because it is taken for granted, that you are alive, and therefore, you don't need to say it or mention it as an answer for the answer of the supposed question, made at the beginning of this preface. No body's perfect.

Any answer of course is expected from you. No one have the power over yourself can limit your imagination or innovation to say what you want or select from inside or outside the list as a response. You had the free will to think and choose. But you did what you did to answer the question posed here, Whatever force I had over you is not important, the most important thing, that you have to think of your life first, then think of stress, anger, anxiety, depression, and fear. Am I right? May be.

People used to conform in their normal life, if they were greeted, they respond. If they were asked, they also respond. If they were called, they also respond. Your response is normal, but what is NOT normal, is to give a response, others expect from you to conform to what they ask for. You have your own personality with different traits from others, you have control of your self and actions. If your personality was of Type A, or Type B. personality, and I knew that about you, I can guess what your answer would be from the above list. I would also guess whither you are open minded or close minded according to some psychologists. I would guess whither you belong to the first in hierarchy or the last in Maslow's model of human needs. Further, I would guess your age, and may be your sex. Believe me, I can guess too many things about you. And I can tell you what you need to cope and how to manage all or one of the FGMs. You don't believe me. OK. It's up to you. As I told you. You are in control of your self, and you think surely, that LIFE itself, Is, and should be the first to think as bringing happiness to your life. Think about it.

This book is very much different from the sixteen books I authored and published, but close to some of my papers presented in professional sociological or psychological or educational conferences. Life satisfaction and happiness in life is an interesting subject. I ask people very simple question, who are you? I made research among Muslims, non

Muslims, Arabs, and non-Arabs, American and non Americans, young adults, males females, middle aged, and old and asked this simple question. Guess what the answers would be. Some gives their names, other group gives their religion, other some say their job, a forth group gives their nationality, still other have different answers, they may give to define themselves by their sex, and finally they may give an answer that they are humans, or else. The question is simple enough to think about. It is not about your name, or religion, or sex, or age, or your job or your nationality. WHO ARE YOU? I used different methods to reach out to people and let them shoose from a list. 99% of the respondents in my research projects where exactly like you. They answer almost the same concepts you picked, or other concepts from the list. So, knowing this, will give you a quality as normal and unique as a member of the people who picked the same as you did. Life is worth everything good in it. Life is the tree where birds come to rest and go. And finally, I bring this quote from China, it reads: The miracle for humans is not to fly in the air, or to walk on the water, but to walk on the earth. However, happiness cannot be determined by walking on the earth. Let me ask this question: Which country do you think is the first on happiness? That means lack of stress and anxiety. A researcher has put together a map of happiness in the world. The map shows that Denmark is the No. 1 destination. Because of health levels, prosperity and education were the strongest determinants of happiness. Money might not guarantee happiness, but it does make a significant contribution when it is spend on healthcare and education. It probably comes as no surprise that Zimbabwe and Burundi come bottom: oddly enough, the USA is placed at 23 and UK at 41 out of 178 countries.

RULES TO DEFEAT
PTSD EPIDEMICS

Our goal in this chapter is to help finding certain rules to have hands on. However it depends on personal moods such as being optimists or pessimists, influence their way of thinking when explaining happiness. Pessimists think that the pain of people greatly exceeds their pleasure; Rousseau was a pessimist who thought that, all things considered, human life was not a valuable gift. Samuel Johnson agreed that we are not born for happiness. In his book The Conquest of Happiness, the philosopher Bertrand Russell (1930-1985) reiterated that most people are unhappy. On the other hand, optimists feel happy and are satisfied with life (Inglehart 1990; Myers 1993).I suggest these thirty rules to deal with stress, and anxiety. Emphasis was put bold, for the core words of each rule. You have to feel that without yourself involved in the treatment, you cannot manage your stress. You have to accept yourself as it is first. And accept all or some of the following 30 rules to tame the PTSD diseases.

1.   Keep your anger under control, and manage it before blowing. Take a long breath, and remember that anger will destroy your all good qualities. Therefore,

after a long breath, talk slowly and in low voice.

2.   Do not make sides in situations arise. For example, don't be over exited in happy occasions or very much sad . You have to accept both situation as a normal part of life. To practice this advice may be difficult for you, so I can give some hints to overcome such difficulty, be patient and count to ten before showing your reaction to occasions happen in front of you. Try it. Count from one to ten slowly. This will give you time to react in a very normal way.

3.   Simplicity is great, makes other people invite you to their circles quickly and easily. Be simple in your life. Do not feel superiority over others. You must try your best to achieve you goal but never blame your self or situations around you. Face your failure bravely and accept it as normal thing people usually do. Every human is NOT perfect, so you.

4.   Managing stress includes abandoning jealousy from your friends, colleagues or anyone else, because jealousy hurt your position in the group

5.   Helping others is a good technique to get rid of stress. It will give you time to think of others and spent time with those who need you. They say, If you see others' troubles, you find your trouble is not the most one.

6.   Don't blame yourself, or punish it. But reward it when it makes good things, and talk with yourself calmly when you feel there was a mistake. Keep the spirit high.

7.   The Money factor cannot be always an important factor for happiness. If you earn it, use it carefully, but not get mad to loose it. They say, money comes, money goes, so why bother. You ar healthy, active and alive.

8.   To coping with stress you must accept that you are unique individual among your peers. Feel like anybody else that you have some good and some bad habits. And search for the good things in your inner self, you will find out what is unique about you. Use paper and pencil and write down what you come up from your brain storming exercise. You will be surprised to find too many unique qualities in yourself.

9.   Get rid of your bad habits, and try not to be addicted to any of them. Cigarette, alcohol, drugs, etc., feel always that these habits are causing the problem not solving it. Reduce it first, by spacing by looking at your watch, you will find that you can control how many times you control such timing. The increase the time space, from one hour to two, the to five, then to eight. Then finally quit.

10.   Time Planning is may be the best way to help you manage stress situations. You will control surprise by planning. Because traumatic surprises cause stress. So you have to manage your time, and follow your daily program, even if it looks simple or empty, after many days you used to it and begin good planning by including activities new to your life.

11.   Priority factor: Develop a habit of making system for priority of things. For example to walk first in the morning or afternoon first, before eating. Or before reading your newspaper, or before going out to buy things from the supermarket. And be specific to do one thing in one time, meaning do not mix two things together and follow your list. Be strict with yourself to follow it. It will be hard to do that at the beginning, but you will find your self that you are

becoming an expert in prioritizing. This will reduce your stress.

12. Be a watcher of anxiety not an owner. If have PDST or panic attacks then always keep in mind that Fear of anxiety is always bigger then fear itself. They say, fear makes the wolf much bigger than itself. And be optimistic rather than pessimistic

13. Accept others as they are, not as you like them to be.

14. Tame the ego in yourself. The ego is may be the main source of anger which leads to stress and negative reactions. Don't let the ego tame you, because you will loose friends. You may satisfy it by negotiating with it. Because selfishness is common to all people, don't show it if you have more than others. Keep it inside, hide it, in other words, control it.

15. Your over expectations from others are major source of stress. This habit will reduce your stress at great level.

16. Think to secure some savings, do not spend all what you got. Try to develop a habit of savings at least 10 %, or 20% of income. This action will

reduce your stress and give you a feeling that you can be financially secure.

17. Do not fly, but face it. Face the problems and explain them logically and calmly. Do not close your mind of discussing it. Train yourself to be involved rather than escaping.

18. Change your routine life. Try to develop a habit of meet new people and building new relationships. Many people who feel shyness or fear of meeting people are apt to build up stress over time. If you are victim of shyness then make habit of talk with yourself first, and then practice to know new people. Begin with your close circle at school, work, or even in a trip. You will be surprised to see that you are not the most person who feels shyness. And people like to talk on any thing, begin with the weather, then something passing through, good or bad. But keep yourself listening more than talking. And talk when it is necessary. So you become more and more involved in talk situations.

19. You have to be in control. If you loose control, then you become like the ball in the soccer game. You have to be the player who shoots the ball, not the ball. You have to control your emotions when making decisions. Try to make

sure, your emotions are second to your mind, not vise versa.

20.   Give options for decisions you have to make, ask yourself what if. Questions, and answer these question mentally not physically. Otherwise you will loose your power to control stress. And it will control you.

21.   Your self esteem should be high. But in control and with guidance. You have to limit your self esteem by knowing your limts. You can help yourself in this case by accepting errors sometimes, and promise yourself to accept successes without bragging.

29.   Use term "we" instead of "I" to give   listeners the intimate feeling to understand you.

22.   Beware of bad company: Select your company away from those who have negative   thinking,   always   talking selfishly about themselves. Or criticizing others for no specific reasons. Do not take people around you for granted, friendship takes sometimes a long time to be built on solid grounds. Therefore, you have to take your time to search for company of positive people who think positively.

23. Try to replace your words you were accustomed to use in your daily routine, pick positive not negative words. For example, instead of stupid, not intelligent is better, you ar not saying the truth, is much better than you are lying, I do not like to see you, instead of I hate to see you. She looks not smart, instead of she looks stupid.

24. Control Your eating habits by organizing times of eating. Healthy mind can reside in healthy body is a general principle, they say in old Arab proverb. Because getting over weight will be a fat factor determine stress for you.

25. Be open minded to receive new ideas, and initiate activities for group games in your vacation times with family members and peers.

26. Read everyday something, short or long stories, magazines, and journals. Reading enhance your understanding of the world around you. You will feel that the world is running around you, and you have to join it. Otherwise you will remain in your cell with no keys.

27. Share your thoughts: Do not hesitate to express your thoughts. Don't make it a habit of closing your personality from others by not sharing stressful thoughts from family or loved ones, because sharing is a great quality to

be a human able to help yourself and cope with stressful situations.
28. Do not wait tomorrow, it is surely coming to be today, and then yesterday. Just wait, and live harmoniously with your close social environmental circle. Your family and practice the principle LET GO.
29. Your belief is your church, pray or mediate a moment of time alone. It is a practice recommended by many doctors. You have to stop doing anything. Just pouse and think for a certain time, five minutes, ten minutes, to half an hour a day. You will find that your knowledge of yourself is increasing by time, and your relations with others is enhanced. I wish you a good Luck.
30. Success can be achieved by You. You now may become an expert in your stress.
So at last, tell yourself that you decided to follow some of the above rules freely as your time permits. You can make your own personal contract. you are responsible to check it every day. And you have the freedom to be angry sometimes, but you have to possess the ability to turn your anger, stress, anxiety and fear into a satisfaction mood in your life. You will be the master of your own actions. You have the control over them, and don't let them take control from you.

Feel strength over them, and you will feel happy to enjoy life.

As you see, there is lot of ways to coping with stress and more techniques for managing it. You suffer from stress lot and try most of these methods and techniques for managing stress If you want to coping with stress then you must change yourself nothing else can relieve you from stress permanently.

حول مطبوعات الموسوعة العربية الأمريكية
ومنشورات معهد إحياء التراث العربي في المهاجر

Arab American Encyclopedia-USA - Hasan Yahya

About the author
Dr. Hasan A. Yahya الدكتور حسن عبدالقادر يحيى

Professor, Dr. Hasan A. Yahya is a Jordania American writer originally born in Palestine. He's the author of American Arab Encyclopedia (AAE), the Honorary Committee Member of the Arab & Muslim Writers Union-(A&MWU), the Dean of the Arab writers in North America, an SME Expert , and president of DryahyaTV. He's an Arab American writer, scholar, poet and retired professor of Sociology. He graduated from Michigan State University with 2 Ph.d degrees. He published 150 books plus (105 Arabic and 45 English & Bilingual), and 500 plus articles on sociology, religion, psychology, politics, poetry, and short stories. Philosophically, his writings concern logic, justice and human rights worldwide. Dr. Yahya is the author of best selling book: Crescentologism: The Moon Theory, and Islam Finds its Way, in English, and 28 Arabic Short Stories in Arabic, all on Amazon, Create-space and Kindle. He's of encyclopedic nature in knowledge, an expert on Race Relations, Arab & Islamic cultures. His main interested in Philosophy, Religion, World affairs and global strategic planning for the purpose of justice and human rights. www.dryahyatv.com From his quotes: "No body is perfect, mentally or physically" and "If people loose their dignity, No one may imagine what they are capable of doing to regain it.

ولد في مجدل يابا من أعمال يافا – فلسطين عام 1944. تلقى علومه الابتدائية في مدرسة بديا الأميرية في الضفة الغربية أيام احتوائها ضمن المملكة الأردنية الهاشمية وتخرج في جامعة بيروت حاملاً

الإجازة في اللغة العربية وآدابها، ودبلوم التأهيل التربوي من كلية القديس يوسف بلبنان، ودبلوم الدراسات العليا (الماجستير) ودكتوراة في الإدارة التربوية من جامعة ولاية ميشيغان بالولايات المتحدة عام 1988، وشهادة الدكتوراه في علم الاجتماع المقارن من الجامعة نفسها عام 1991. عمل في التدريس والصحافة الأدبية. ومنصرف إلى الكتابة في علوم كثيرة تخص علمي النفس والاجتماع والتنمية البشرية ، ألف ونشر العديد من المقالات والكتب باللغتين العربية والإنجليزية ، وله ست مجموعات قصصية وست كتب للأطفال ، وأربع دواوين شعرية باللغتين أيضا. وهو الآن أستاذ متقاعد في جامعة ولاية ميشيغان. وهو عضو جمعية الكتاب العرب والمسلمين في أمريكا الشمالية ومؤسس الموسوعة العربية الأمريكية في الولايات المتحدة ضمن مشروع إحياء التراث العربي في بلاد المهجر .

مؤلفاته:

Arab American Encyclopedia Publications
منشورات الموسوعة العربية الأمريكية
Dr. Hasan Yahya Books - كتب الدكتور: د حسن يحيى

كتب (بالعربية والإنجليزية) ، قام بنشرها الدكتور حسن يحيى ضمن مشروعه: إحياء التراث العربي في المهجر ، بالتعاون مع الموسوعة العربية الأمريكية التي أسسها أيضا لهذا الغرض ومعهد البحوث الإدارية ومطابع شركة البركان وتلفزيون الدكتور يحيى في الولايات المتحدة :

The Arab American Encyclopedia Publications:
In English:
1. Moon Flowers: Poems, Tales & Politics
2. Poetry Diwan: Love, Fears & Hopes
3. Crescentology: A Theory Of Conflict Management And Cultural Normalization
4. Crescentologism: The Moon Theory
5. Brief Arab & Muslim Ethics: For Non-Arabic Speakers (Bilingual)
6. The Beast In Me America: Arabic Folklore, Tales, Stories, & Poetry
7. Personality & Stress Management: A New Theory

8. Arab Palestinian & Jews: Sociological Aproach
9. Legal Adultery: Sexuality & World Cultures
10. Crescentologism: The Moon Theory
11. Islam: Finds Its Way
12. 30 Tales From Faraway Land: Middle Eastern
13. Brief Islamic History (bilingual)
14. Jesus Christ Speaks Arabic
15. فن أدبي جديدFan Adabi Jadid (bilingual)
16. Protocols of Zion: Trilingual : Spnaish, English & Arabic
17. Prophets Saga: from Adam to Muhammad
18. Al-Akhlaq al-Islamiyyah (Bilingual)
19. Quotes: Love & Humor (Bilingual)
20. Jesus is Different the Prophets History
21. 50 Short Stories (55 words)-Bilingual
22. The Intruder: Bilingual
23. *Alisha and Other Stories.*
24. 70 Very Short Stories (English)
25. *Short Stories from World Literature (Bilingual)*
26. 65 stories for Children 3-12 , (English)
27. Occupation and Other Stories from World Literature –English
28. 85 Fables & Tales for Children 3 to 12 (English)
29. *Naji al-Ali Art Show.* A Palestinian Artist *Ann Mary Thatcher*
30. Princess Imagination: A New Design Novel (English)
31. Al-Hariri Assemblies (Maqamat al-Hariri (English)
32. Water, Population and Conflict in the Middle East.
33. *Princess Diana Still Alive, A New Novel Design. Ann Mary Thatcher.*
34. *Nietzsche On Christianity*
35. *Bertrand Russell: Roads to Freedom*
36. *The Dangers of the GMS:Slideshow & Presebtation*
37. *Ernest HemingwaySuicide Story*
38. *Brief Management: Theories & Applications.*
39. *I Have the Right to be Angry*
40. *FBI Madness Storm , One Act Play*

أما مقالاته فتزيد على الخمسمائة مقال باللغتين العربية والإنجليزية وهي منشورة على الإنترنت ، وتم جمع بعضها في كتبه الإنجليزية والعربية كل في مجاله .

www.ingramcontent.com/pod-product-compliance
Lightning Source LLC
Chambersburg PA
CBHW051953280526
45789CB00009B/3273